STREET MARKETS

STREET MARKETS

Written & Illustrated by
CAROL L. COHEN

Grosset & Dunlap
A National General Company

Publishers   New York

To Graham

"If you have two loaves of bread,
Keep one to feed your hunger,
& sell the other to buy
hyacinths for your soul."
                    -Chinese proverb

·Acknowledgments·

For their help in the preparation of this manuscript I would like to thank Martha Alexander, Graham E. Becker, Kathryn Lynch Burk, Nancy Brooks, Carl Crosbie, Sheldon Fogelman, John Friend, Joan Glueckman, Leo Lerman, Edith Raymond Locke, Anne Klein, Esta Marshall, Maurizio di Puolo, Atha Tehon & Barry Zaid.

·CONTENTS·

·Introduction·

There have always been peddlers selling their wares in the street & there's still no more friendly, colorful or varied way of shopping than an outdoor street market. It's noisy, unpredictable, fascinating— & always very much a part of the city life. Here treasures & junk are mixed together & spread out cafeteria style for you to browse & wander through at your leisure. Go & find: an antique pocket watch with your initials already on it; a 30's dancing dress you can wear tonight; or a 12-piece set of Victorian silverware at ⅕ the price of new!

Go chat up a dealer! Bargain!
Start a collection!
Eat street foods!
Have fun! Fun! Fun!

·Hints Before You Go·

  This book was designed in the hope
that it will be carried to market,
consulted as a guide & made more useful
by your own notes. It's by no means a
last-word tome on antiques, but rather
tidbits of information, history &
identification clues picked up from
dealers' chat, reading & just looking.
It would be impossible to show every
item available in all the markets, but
the selection is an indication of
what can be found in each city.
Related items have been grouped together
to show you the possibilities of collecting.
Prices have been omitted since they
change constantly, but particular
bargains are noted. Almost none of
the articles shown are the stuff
museums are made of, so they shouldn't
be exorbitant. They range in price
anywhere from 5¢ to $5.00, with

most under $25. But whatever you decide to spend, it's hoped that <u>Street Markets</u> will give you a taste of the delights awaiting the traveler/collector.

Be Sure to check the days & hours each market is open before you go. Don't be disappointed!

Better Save your Strength for the market. Take a Taxi!

Remember the marked price is almost never the final price. Bargain!

Comparative Shop before you buy! If you're Looking for one particular item check the price at various stalls.

Don't be afraid to ask the dealer questions!

What to Wear

Old Clothes - it's better to pass as a native or a dealer.

Old Shoes - it's muddy & in winter cold & wet.

·What to Say & How to Bargain·

You: Show interest, pick up item with care & examine (like a pro).

Dealer: Will often supply the 1st price without your even asking!

You: "It's a bit steep, that's dear, could you drop it a bit? Knock something off it? C'est trop (Fr.). Sono troppo (It.)"

Dealer: Comes down some....

You: "Is that your best on it?"

Dealer: _____

You: Last resort, turn & start to walk away....

Dealer: (In Fr./It.) will grab your arm & say "How much?"

You: Name your price, usually ½ off the 1st price in France or Spain, $\frac{1}{10}$ off in England, $\frac{2}{3}$ in Italy, etc.

You & Dealer: Haggle up & down, both pretend to compromise, drink a cup of tea....

NOTE ✳ Never insult a dealer's wares or he may refuse to sell you!

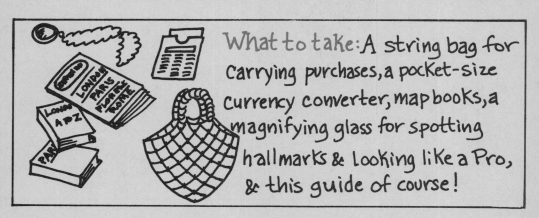

What to take: A string bag for carrying purchases, a pocket-size currency converter, map books, a magnifying glass for spotting hallmarks & looking like a Pro, & this guide of course!

LONDON

BERMONDSEY STREET S.E.1

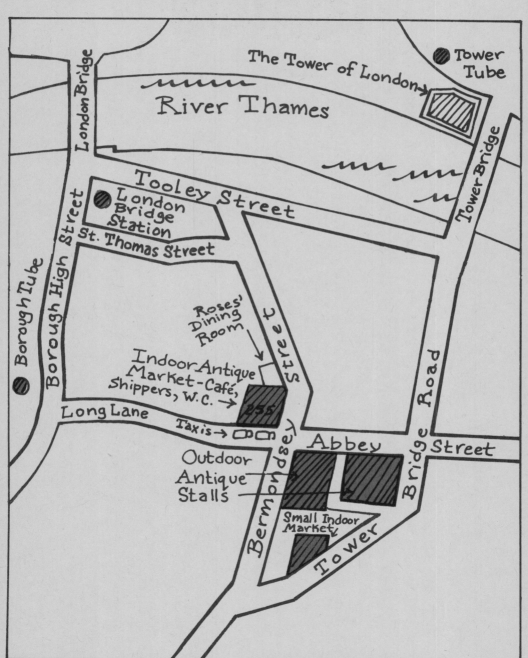

The Tower of London →

Tower Tube

River Thames

London Bridge

Tower Bridge

Tooley Street

London Bridge Station

St. Thomas Street

Borough High Street

Borough Tube

Roses' Dining Room

Indoor Antique Market—Café, Shippers, W.C. →

255

Bermondsey Street

Long Lane

Taxis →

Abbey Street

Bridge Road

Outdoor Antique Stalls

Small Indoor Market

Tower

Bermondsey Street   "Caledonian Market" is on Bermondsey Square between Tower Bridge Road & Bermondsey street.

Transport: Tube- take the Northern line to Borough station-but it's best to take a taxi.

Days & Hours: Fridays only, 6am - 2 pm.

Layout: Over 350 stalls in the outdoor section & 100 more at 255, Long Lane, the indoor market.

Bermondsey is a large open-air antique/junk market where all the dealers go on Friday to stock up for their Saturday sales. They come at 6 in the morning, flashlights in hand, like detectives in the night, looking for the ultimate find. The stallholders come from far & wide, after a week of buying at auctions, fairs, house clearances & spend the night setting up their wares, then open up at 5 or 6. Furniture is sold from the backs of vans from midnight on. Bermondsey is where the greatest volume of goods & $ change hands, so go early for the best buys in silver, Victoriana, clocks, china, furniture, bric-a-brac.

When buying Silver Frames Look for holes in the raised surfaces caused by years of polishing. Run your fingers along the edges, feeling for serrations. Damages are expensive to repair & detract from the value

Silver Flatware-

Are all the pieces there & do they match? Check for hallmarks on the ring between the blade & the handle. If uncertain, ask for a detailed receipt.

Silver Candlesticks-

Look for wear along the edges, dents, knocks. Is the decoration crisp & sharp? Have the sticks been repaired? Breathe on them to dull the surface shine to show up repairs, joins, hallmarks.

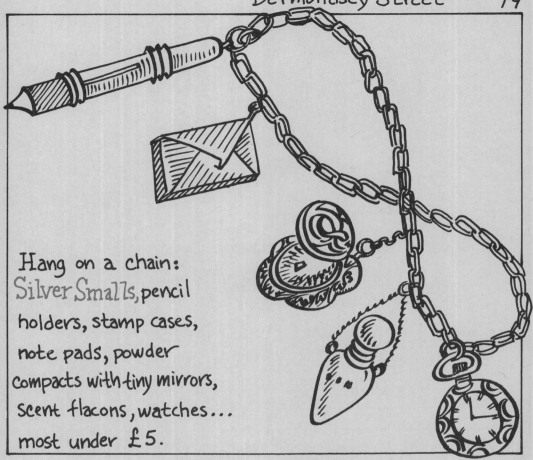

Hang on a chain:
Silver Smalls, pencil
holders, stamp cases,
note pads, powder
compacts with tiny mirrors,
scent flacons, watches...
most under £5.

Buy the REAL THING! English Sterling Silver is always
Hallmarked! Look for 4 marks: the maker's initials;
the standard mark (a lion) indicating the sterling quality;
the town or "hall" mark; & the year letter. English
sterling silver must be a fixed standard of 925
parts silver & 75 parts copper. Bring a magnifying
glass & a hallmark identification book.

Have a Victorian tea party with Sheffield Plate - a sandwich of copper between two sheets of silver plate. Popular in 1800-1840 when middle-class Victorians wanted to own tea sets like the rich, & copied the expensive sterling sets by this cheaper method. If the plate is worn off in spots, do not replate - This is part of its beauty.

Silver Caddy Spoons - to measure out tea when it was still a luxury. They are short-handled with a wide bowl. Look for unusual shapes such as jockey caps & check hallmarks.

Silver Tea Strainers - used so you didn't get a mouth full of grouts. More valuable if it still has its stand.

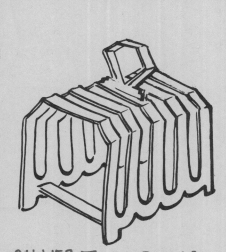

SILVER Toast Racks-
amusing items to collect
& good for holding
bills, letters, photos.
Inexpensive.

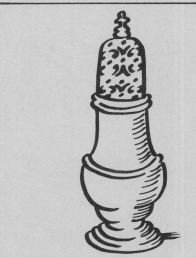

SILVER Sugar Dredgers
were used to sprinkle
sugar on your
crumpets at high tea.

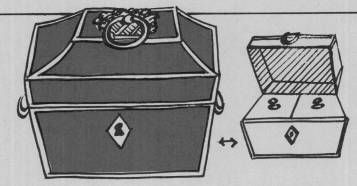

Tea first came to England in the 17th C & by the 18th
was already a habit though an expensive one & a
luxury. So it was kept under lock & key in Tea Caddies
named after the Malayan measure of weight, the "Kati,"
equaling 1-2 lbs. Look for two storage bins inside for China
& India tea. The more elaborate have a mixing bowl as well.

Lots of Copper Kettles, molds, saucepans from the Victorian Kitchen. Copper looks lovely but may need retinning & elbow grease. Buy at the stalls & also from the Tattoo Man in Portobello Road, £4 & up.

Horse Brasses were used as ornaments on horses' harnesses. If old they can be valuable. Check the back - if they are pitted & lumpy they're newly made.

Brass Door Knockers & other door fittings. Most are reproductions of earlier styles. Pick them up - old brass is heavier than new brass.

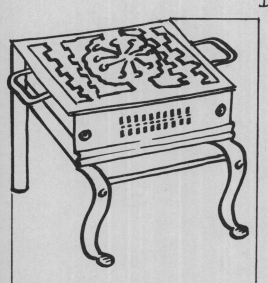

A VICTORIAN Footman in brass or cast iron. Used as a kind of trivet in front of the fireplace to warm wet feet or a pot of water- Look for cabriole legs.

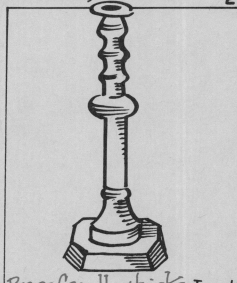

Brass Candlesticks- Look for square bases. They should show wear on the underside. Old sticks were rough cast & heavy. New ones are lighter & smooth-bottomed.

Copper Coal Scuttles
Look for holes where the shovel went in at the lip, loose handles, splits near the base. If they're old they should show the hard wear of daily use. Should be helmet-shaped.

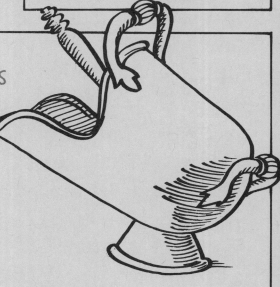

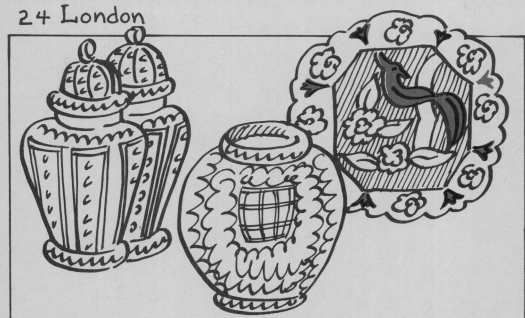

Some tips on buying Oriental China:

Check if it's all there. Is the lid missing? Are there cracks or chips on the base or edges? Old china is prone to damage & often top-heavy pieces were kept on pedestals in Victorian homes. As the maid went by with her mop many a fine vase "bit the dust," so don't be put off by minor damages.

Types to look for:

Blue & White - traditional patterns of birds & trees - the darker & smudgy blues are made recently.

Cantonese - light green ground with butterflies & figures going around.

Imari - bright floral patterns taken from Japanese brocades.

Satsumi - bright colors, gilt & a coarse texture.

Lustreware 1st came to Spain with Moors & Josiah Wedgwood revived the art in England in the 1800's. The silver, gold & coppery glazes were made to imitate the real thing.

19th C Doulton salt-glaze stoneware jugs with raised hunting scenes, windmills & "Toby" figures, were used for holding hot punch because they retain the heat.

Wedgwood is the name of the maker of many types of china, such as: Jasper ware- lavender & white with classical designs. Basalt- a raised pattern on matt black. Creamware- plain white china.

When the clock strikes 12... from midnight on Furniture is sold from the backs of vans at reasonable prices.

Pick up a copy of—The Lyle Official Antiques Review for an excellent source of current prices, dates & hallmarks. Buy it at the "Caff" in the Antique Market, 255, Long Lane, or any London bookshop.

To pass as a Dealer or Shipper, bring a little black notebook to record purchases, a large satchel to carry them in, price tags & a magnifying glass.

Start off Market day with:

One on a raft

cuppa tea an' a bacon wad

Bangers

Liver-Tomato-Chips

Dripping bread

All at the caff
or
Rose's Dining Room.

20 Bermondsey Street.

JOYCES

For jellied
eels & mashed

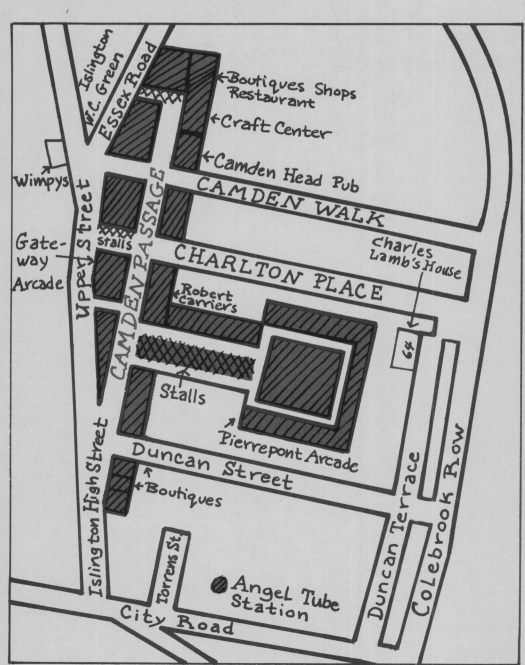

LONDON BOROUGH OF ISLINGTON
CAMDEN
PASSAGE N.1

Islington W.C. Green

Essex Road

←Boutiques Shops
Restaurant

←Craft Center

←Camden Head Pub

Wimpys→

Upper Street

CAMDEN PASSAGE

CAMDEN WALK

stalls

Gate-
way
Arcade

CHARLTON PLACE

Charles
Lamb's House

64

←Robert
Carriers

Stalls

Pierrepont Arcade

Islington High Street

Duncan Street

Duncan Terrace

Colebrook Row

←Boutiques

Torrens St.

Angel Tube
Station

City Road

Camden Passage is in Islington High street, N.1.
Transport: Take the Northern Line to Angel station
Bus: 4a, 19, 30, 38, 43, 73, 171, 172.
Days & Hours: Market on Wednesday & Saturday.
Most shops open all week.
Layout: Over 100 shops & stalls & arcades
down a cobbled-stone walk.

Camden Passage, once a quiet little 18th c back-
water at the Angel, Islington, is a charming cobbled street
full of boutiques, stalls & arcades. Surrounded by Georgian
houses, Charles Lamb's house & historic Islington Green,
the Passage has become a fashionable area to browse, shop
& walk about in. The market was started in 1960 & is
ideal for decorators, dealers & collectors of Victoriana,
Art Nouveau & Art Deco, silver, jewelry, clocks, militaria
& nautical items & decorative items of all kinds. The
shops are open all week & the market is held on Saturday
(when the locals & tourists come) & on Wednesday (when the
dealers come) so for bargains go Wednesdays.

All VICTORIANA dates from the reign of Queen Victoria in England, 1837-1901, when there was a change in style from the simple elegance of the Regency to a more fussy, cluttered style, along with a shift in the moral climate from decadence & opulence to a return of the family, respectability & sentimentality.

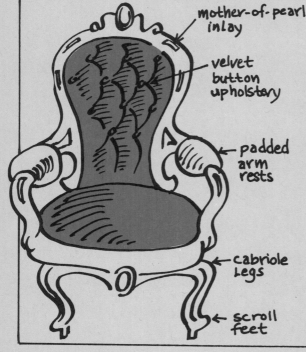

mother-of-pearl inlay

velvet button upholstery

padded arm rests

cabriole legs

scroll feet

In VICTORIAN Furniture comfort took precedence over aesthetics. Look for the extensive use of padded upholstery & large heavy solid furniture, richly carved & polished. Can be found in all the London markets.

Victorian Ladies kept themselves busy with all kinds of needlework & had workbox-treasure-troves full of delightful Sewing Aids.

Beware Reproductions!

VICTORIAN Staffordshire dogs, cats, sheep, cottages, flatback figures & portraits. Look for a fine network of tiny cracks or "crazing," soft faded colors. Bottom rims should be unglazed.

ART NOUVEAU Accessories

In the 1890's it became fashionable to adorn bric-a-brac-lamps, mirrors, ashtrays made of pottery, metal or glass - with "petite femmes." Art Nouveau items are characterized by asymmetry & plantlike swirling convolutions. Available in all the markets.

ART NOUVEAU Silver Scent Flacon

Look for forms such as women with swirling flowing hair, flower & leaf motifs (1890-1910).

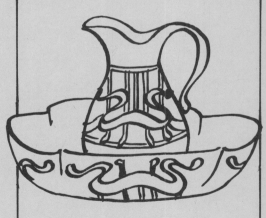

Jug & Basin with Art Nouveau designs.

Make sure basin & jug have the same matching pattern & no cracks or chips on the lip or handle.

ART DECO Accessories

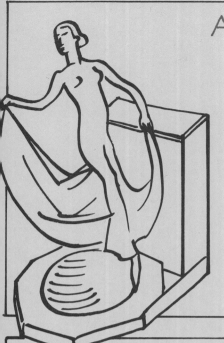

Stylized dancing figures in ceramic or soft metal frequently turn up as '30's ashtrays, lamps or cigarette lighters, probably inspired by chorus girl line-ups from the movies.

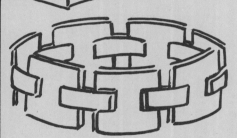

Geometric Jewelry

in the "new" synthetics: bakelite, chrome, plastic, celluloid. The Art Deco style (1914-1940) was influenced by the Bauhaus, Cubism & the discovery of King Tut's tomb.

Powder Compacts, Cigarette Cases & Jewelry,

all enamel on silvery grounds in geometric patterns at London's Art Deco specialist, Chiu, 10 Charlton Place.

Act of Parliament Clock

usually kept at Inns & public buildings to keep patrons informed of the time after Parliament passed an act in 1797 levying a tax on all persons owning clocks or watches. A specialty at: Strike One, 1a Camden Walk.

Magic Lanterns

were used by Victorians to show slides (the first movies). Check to see that all the parts are there & that it still works. Other machines available as well, such as: early cameras, music boxes, telescopes, etc.

Brass Miner's Lamp

as well as lanterns of
all kinds in all the
markets. They can be
hooked up as lamps.

Antique Firearms

Uniforms
Edged Weapons
Militaria of all kinds at:
#3, Phelps Cottage
Angel Armoury
The American Shop

Collect Toy Soldiers

Look for complete sets of 8 or more in their
original boxes. They should be lead, without
damages or chipped paint.

a noble Student of Oxford

Prints old & new of all kinds at reasonable prices. Many prints found loose now began as illustrations in bound books. At Finbar MacDonnell, 17, Camden Passage. Also try The Corner Cupboard for Victorian prints.

Lots of "Interior Decorator's Items" such as hat stands or Screens, not necessarily antiques or useful, but good to fill up an empty corner.

Play an old windup Gramophone. Also old records of the 30's-50's & sheet music at D.S. Levey, 45, Camden Passage.

At lunchtime head for the pub—

Bangers & Mash

Steak & Kidney Pud

Crumpet
(real English muffin)

Pork Sausage Rolls

Cottage Pie

Really good snacks in a Victorian setting at the Camden Head Pub, Camden Walk.

Robert Carrier's for a posh lunch or dinner — reserve ahead. Or go round the corner to the cook shop for cold gourmet foods, kitchen cookware & cookbooks.

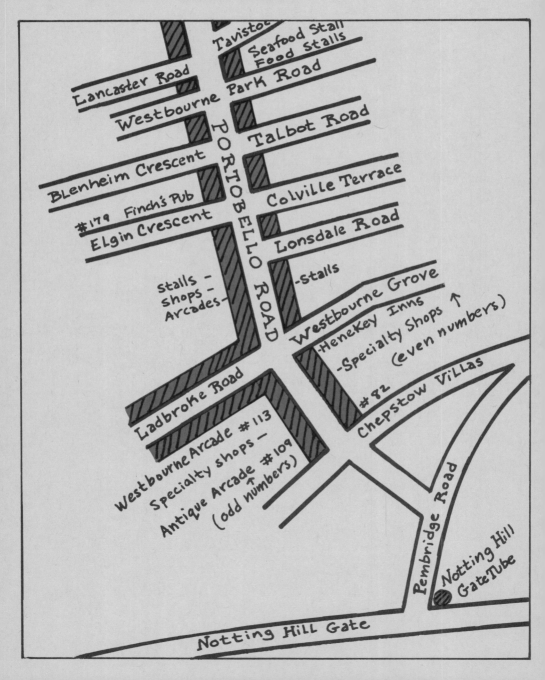

The Royal Borough of Kensington.
PORTOBELLO ROAD. W.10

Tavistoc
Seafood Stall
Food Stalls
Lancaster Road
Westbourne Park Road
PORTOBELLO ROAD
Talbot Road
Blenheim Crescent
Colville Terrace
#179   Finch's Pub
Elgin Crescent
Lonsdale Road
Stalls —
Shops —
Arcades—
-Stalls
Westbourne Grove
-Henekey Inns
-Specialty Shops ↑
(even numbers)
Ladbroke Road
#82
Chepstow Villas
Westbourne Arcade #113
Specialty shops —
Antique Arcade #109
↑
(odd numbers)
Pembridge Road
Notting Hill Gate Tube
Notting Hill Gate

Portobello Road market is located off Pembridge Road & extends down below Tavistock Road, W.10.
Transport: Take the Central Line to Notting Hill Gate station. Bus: 27, 28, 31, 52.
Days & Hours: Saturday 7:30 a.m. - 6 p.m.
Layout: Stalls, shops, arcades & street vendors stretch down one long street with some side streets of shops.

Portobello Road was named after the British naval battle in 1739 at Portobello in South America. The road stretches for about a mile, so start at the top at Chepstow Villas, where the posh specialist shops & arcades are. At Westbourne Grove the cheaper stalls begin. At Elgin Crescent are the food & junk stalls & prices drop further. Don't just look at the shops, but notice the people out for their Saturday promenade. The road is chock-a-block with tourists, locals, dealers, hippies, street vendors & muscians, organ grinders & don't miss the Tattoo Man selling his pots & pans. Because of the heavy tourist traffic prices tend to be high. Go early for bargains. You'll find in Portobello: Victoriana, Art Nouveau & Deco, furniture, brass & copper, silver, nautical items, old clothes & all kinds of smalls.

Everything ship shape - Nautical Equipment of all
Kinds: early instruments, figureheads, maps, lamps,
portholes at Trad #67, Jan's #69 & the shops & arcades.

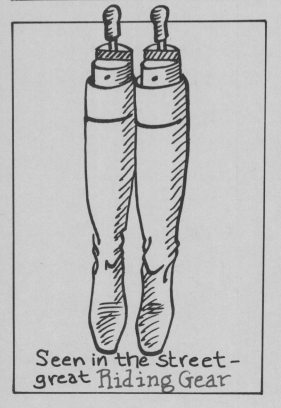

Seen in the street -
great Riding Gear

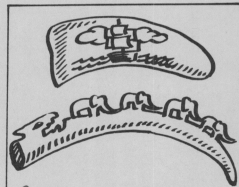

Scrimshaw is engraved
or carved ivory from
whale tooth, rhino horn,
walrus or elephant tusk.
If old it should be
slightly yellowed.

Old Clothes & Costumes of all periods & styles. Go through stalls in the street.

£1.

Military Gear from the Last war at #84, Portobello.

CORONATION

KING VIII EDWAR

There are two types of Commemorative China:
1) Commemorating royalty & historical anniversaries such as the 50 years since the battle of Waterloo.
2) commemorating famous people such as Lord Nelson.

Pub Signs & Trade Mirrors

Look out for reproductions - many are made today! Old ones should be faded.

Pub Measures

come in sets from ½ gallon down to a tablespoon. "Repros" are often more dented than the real thing.

Silver Drinking Flasks

Be sure the cup matches the top & both are hallmarked. Is the cork in good condition? Look for splits at the seams.

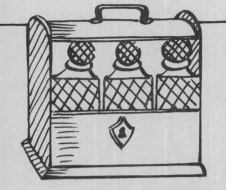

Tantalus for Decanters

Was kept under lock & key so the servants wouldn't steal the master's drink. It should have the key & be in working order. Decanters should all match & not be chipped.

Keeping wine & spirits in cut-glass decanters required Bottle Tickets to distinguish the contents. They were made in silver, gold, porcelain or enamel.

Toby Jugs

are used for pouring beer, & date from the late 18th C on up to today. They are modern if they say "Made in England" on the bottom.

Automated Doll
in a basket. Arms
& legs move as the
carriage is pulled. Dates
from about 1880.
Also French &
German dolls, English
wax dolls at:
Carol Stanton, #109

Scots Pebble Jewelry
When Queen Victoria was
spending her summers at
Balmoral Castle in Scotland,
kilt pins became all the
rage. In silver, malachite,
agate, granite, etc.

**Silver-capped glass
Scent Bottles** from the
Victorian dressing table
in all sizes, shapes & colors.
Make sure the glass stopper
is still intact & the
cap closes tightly.

Small Boxes of all kinds in silver, enamel, tortoise shell, papier mâché, used to hold rouge, powder, bonbons, patches (beauty marks) snuff & medicine. Be sure hinges open & close properly.

Music Boxes

Swiss watchmakers perfected music boxes in the early 1800's & the French put the Swiss works in automated dolls. Seen at Graham Webb, #93.

Usually thought an English invention, Teddy Bears were first made when President Teddy Roosevelt refused to shoot a small bear cub who crossed his firing line on a hunting trip in 1902. The publicity gave him his nickname & a new toy for children all over the world. In all the markets.

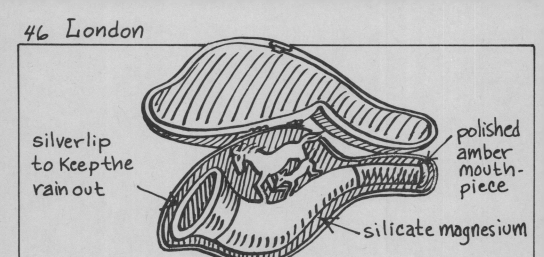

silver lip to keep the rain out

polished amber mouth-piece

silicate magnesium

Meerschaum Pipes are made of a porous material that absorbs nicotine so that the more the pipe is smoked the more it changes color from the original white to ambers & browns. Popular 1800-1860. The carved part is often an animal, a naked Lady or a portrait head.

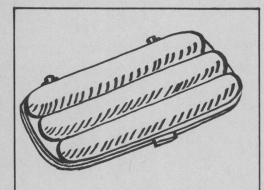

Silver Cigar Cases
Look for the silver hallmark. Make sure hinges & catch work properly. Date from the 1920s-30s.

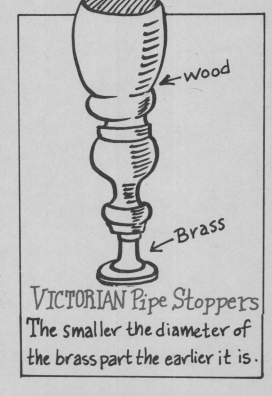

← Wood

← Brass

VICTORIAN Pipe Stoppers
The smaller the diameter of the brass part the earlier it is.

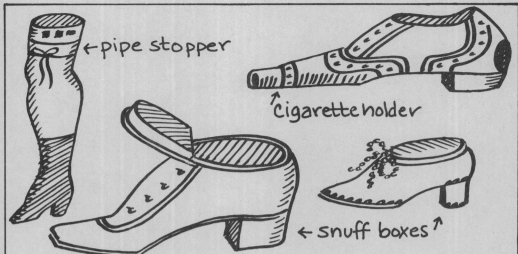

← pipe stopper

↑ cigarette holder

← snuff boxes ↑

Since a lady's foot was rarely seen in Victorian times, it was looked upon with sexual overtones. All kinds of Smoking Accessories were made in the shape of shoes, feet & legs as match boxes, snuff boxes, pipe stoppers, etc. & kept in the gents' smoking room.

Silver Match Boxes are plentiful & cheap in all the markets- Look for hallmarks on the inside rim (see arrow) & a striker along the side. Can be used to hold pills, stamps, coins.

Bring a Basket, a shopping cart or an old pram to carry your purchases.

HENEKEYS GARDEN

Rest your feet awhile & have a beer in the garden at the corner of Westbourne & Portobello.

CERES

269A for organic grains & healthfoods - Check the bulletin board for notices of cheap trips to Morocco & cottages in Wales.

FINCH'S for

At the corner of Elgin Crescent & Portobello.

Stop in the street for the best snacks

JELLIED EELS
TAKE A CARTON HOME WITH YOU!

SHELL FISH
ALL-COOKED FOOD
TO EAT HERE
OR
TAKE AWAY

WHELKS

COCKLES

vinegar

Cheese & cucumber sandwiches
& other English snacks at #131

BEST 5 N.P.

FRESH FRUIT

10 p at
street corners

HOVIS

Sausages, Bread, cheese
from the Deli at 243.
Or make your own Lunch
with goodies from the street stalls.

CITY OF 🛡 LONDON
CUTLER
STREET *E.I.*

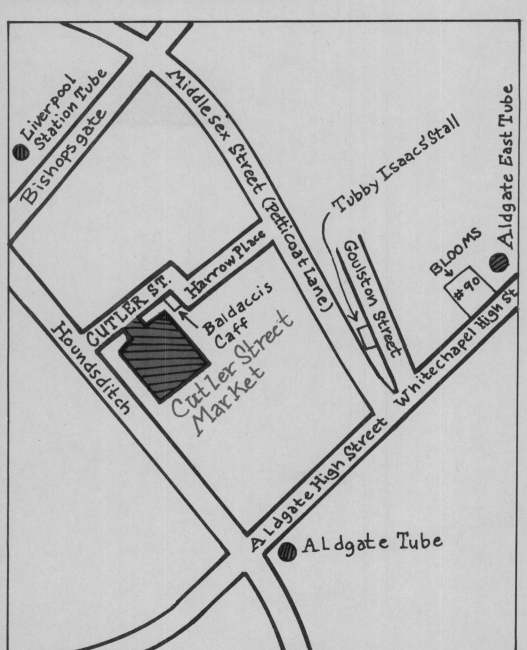

Liverpool Station Tube

Bishopsgate

Middlesex Street (Petticoat Lane)

Tubby Isaacs' Stall

Aldgate East Tube

Harrow Place

CUTLER ST.

Goulston Street

BLOOMS

#90

Baldacci's Caff

Houndsditch

Cutler Street Market

Whitechapel High St

Aldgate High Street

Aldgate Tube

Cutler Street Market is in a little square off
Cutler Street around the corner from Middlesex
Street (Petticoat Lane Market) & Houndsditch Road.
Transport: Tube - take the Circle Line to Aldgate.
Days & Hours: Sundays only, 7am - 1 pm
Layout: about 50 open-air stalls tucked into a
square surrounded by factories & warehouses in the
East End.

Cutler Street Market - Queen Elizabeth I decreed by
an Act of Parliament that there must be a jewelers'
market in the city of London. It was first in Duke
Street till it was bombed in World War II, when it moved
to Cutler Street in 1943. One of the few Cockney
markets left, it is made up of the old school of
dealers who've been in the trade for years & will
drive a hard but fair bargain. They specialize in fine
jewelry, watches, silver (Georgian & Victorian) & coins
(it's THE coin market in London), plus the usual
antique bric-a-brac. Go for authentic atmosphere &
good bargains.

All kinds of Watches - gold, silver, pinchbeck, plate, repeaters, hunters, 8-day winders, Verge. Most will be in working condition. For Victorian watches, don't forget to ask for the key!

Or make your own with - Watch Parts: springs, faces, hands, chains, etc.

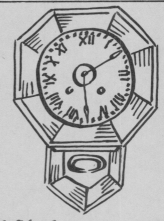

Wall Clocks (used in schools). Look for mahogany cases with enamel faces. Check for cracks & chips on dial, especially around the key hole.

Long Case Clocks or "grandfather" clocks are common in all the markets. Look for brass or painted faces. The price depends on the attractiveness of the case, the size (smaller clocks are more expensive) & the maker's name on the dial or case. Check that the clock is in perfect working order & that keys & pendulum are supplied.

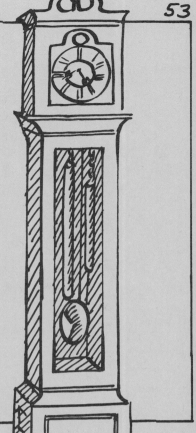

Brass Carriage Clocks were so named because they were taken on long coach journeys. It's unusual to find one today with its original case. Check that the clock is running & that it has glass sides & a glass window at the top.

Chains in gold, silver, pinchbeck, plate. If solid gold or silver, each link should be hallmarked. Check the weight, as the chains are sold by the pound. Also check the length & strength of the links by running them through your fingertips, looking at each link for wear. Links with an etched design are worth more.

Gold Bangles

Check the carats:
9 is usual
15 is Victorian
18 is Georgian
The more attractive the design of the bangle the more valuable it is.

Silver Lockets

Look for the hallmark on each half. The locket should open & close properly & have no splits or holes. Look for chasing design on the cover - avoid initials. The larger & heavier the locket the more expensive.

Mourning Jewelry

After Queen Victoria's husband, Prince Albert, died in 1861, she & all those around her dressed in mourning for the rest of her reign. Black enameled or jet jewelry became the trend & Victorians wore locks of their loved ones' hair in lockets, brooches & pins.

In the 1850's Cameos became THE souvenir to bring home from trips abroad. Usually of a classical subject, they are cut in relief on gem stones or shells. Look for fine detail in the carving of the eyes, nose, hair, etc. The finer the detail & the more interesting the scene the more valuable the piece (Bring your magnifying glass.)

Decorative Pot Lids are tops of jars of fishpaste, meat paste, hair dressing & other Victorian products. "Repros" have duller colors & finish, are flatter, larger & have thick rims.

Battersea Boxes, made of enamel on copper, are very rarely perfect & almost always chipped. Real ones have spotty mirrors inside. Where there's a crack look for the copper underneath as later copies tend to be brass. Boxes with pictures are more desirable than those with mottos.

Silver Vinaigrettes Watch out for new grills replacing old ones or converted pill boxes. Look for hallmarks on the grill as well as on the box. Watch for splits & holes in the corners & hinges.

gilt

Sets of *Georgian* Berry Spoons are frequently seen in the market. Look for clear hallmarks & wear on the front end of the bowl in addition to crispness of design.

Georgian Cream Jugs

should be helmet-shaped & have classical, simple lines resting on 3 legs. Check that the hallmarked part has not been married to another later part which is NOT hallmarked! Look for the leopard's head with crown.

For Outstanding Service - Decorations
Take your pick of medals, badges, helmet
& belt plates - at all the London markets.

Ducats, Drachmas, Silver
dollars. Coins were
invented in the 7th c B.C.
& have been changing
hands ever since. A
large selection for
the numismatic. Also
paper money.

Gold Sovereign Rings
& Pendants made from
old coins. It's really like
buying a lump of gold - get
a receipt guaranteeing
that coins are genuine,
22-carat gold & Look for
a gold hallmark on the shank.

On cold mornings go round to the caff...

for a "cuppa" & listen in on dealers' chat.

OR

OR For the best Kosher Deli in London try Salt (corn) Beef on Rye

potato Latkes

90, Whitechapel High Street.

ALSO IN LONDON—

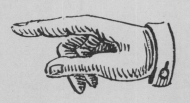

Some other Outdoor Street Markets:

Blackheath Antique Market, Strathendon Road, SE 3, saturdays - books, coins, bric-a-brac, etc.

East Street off Walworth Road, SE 16, sundays - a large junk section in a food market.

Farrington Road Book Market, EC 1, monday through saturday - old books, manuscripts, prints.

Leather Lane, Holborn, EC 1, monday through saturday - clothes, food, household items, etc.

Marylebone Antique Market, 43, Crawford street, W1, monday through saturday - a broad selection of bric-a-brac, furniture, jewelry etc.

Petticoat Lane, Middlesex street, E 1, Sundays - junk old & new, clothes old & new, etc.

Royal Standard Antiques Market, Vanburgh Park, SE 3, saturdays - a wide variety of antiques.

Vallance Road, E 1, sundays - a vast selection of junk stalls.

Some Indoor Markets (These tend to be more expensive than the outdoor markets):

Antique Bazaar, 6, Church street, NW8,

daily - small market with general stock.

The Antique Hypermarket, 26 - 40 Kensington High street, monday through saturday - large posh market with specialist dealers.

Antique Supermarket, 3, Barrett street, W1, daily - a broad selection of antiques.

Bond Street Antique Market, 124, Bond street, W1, mondays through saturday - posh specialist stalls.

Chelsea Antique, 245 Kings Road, SW3, monday through saturday - a large general market.

Chancery Lane Safe Deposit & The London Silver Vaults Ltd, Chancery House, 53, Chancery Lane, WC2 - mostly silver, gems & jewelry.

Some Antiques Areas (There's hardly a street or road in London without its own junk or antique shop!):

- Davies Street, W1.
- Jermyn StreetSW1.
- Mount Street, W1.
- New Bond Street, W1 - for posh shops.
- Fulham Road, SW10.
- Kings Road, SW3 - the far end.
- Pimlico Road, SW1 - for unusual decorator's items.
- Brompton Road, SW3.

Antiques Areas (cont.)

Kensington Church Street W8.

Shippers & Packers: For a complete list of shippers as well as other useful information buy in London "Nicholson's Collectors' London" for 10p., Robert Nicholson Publications. Antique Shippers Ltd. is located at #255, in the Bermondsey Antique Market, Long Lane.

Collections to See:

The big general collections — British Museum, Great Russell Street WC1. The Victoria & Albert Museum, Cromwell Road, SW7. The Wallace Collection, Hertford House, Manchester House W1.

Arms & Armor — The Tower of London

Clocks & Watches — Science Museum, Exhibition Road SW7

Furnishings — Bethnal Green Museum, Cambridge Heath Road, E2. Fenton House, Hempstead Grove NW3.

Oriental — Percival David Foundation, 53 Gordon Square WC1

Nautical — National Maritime Museum, Romney Road SE10

Silver & Gold — Goldsmiths Hall, Foster Lane WC2. The Tower of London, Tower Hill EC3.

Toys & Novelties — Kew Palace, Kew, Surrey. Pollock's Toy Museum, 1 Scala Street W1. London Museum, Kensington Palace, Kensington Gardens W8.

Victoriana — William Morris Gallery, Forest Road E17.

NOTES

Names, Addresses of Dealers, Shops,
Restaurants, Prices paid, etc.

NOTES

PARIS

MARCHÉ AUX PUCES

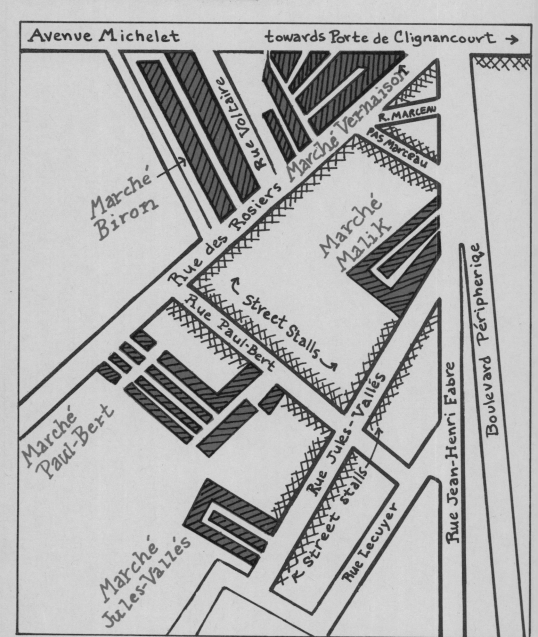

Avenue Michelet   towards Porte de Clignancourt →

Rue Voltaire

Marché Vernaison

R. MARCEAU

PAS Marceau

Marché Biron

Rue des Rosiers

Marché Malik

Boulevard Péripherige

← Street Stalls →

Rue Paul-Bert

Marché Paul-Bert

Rue Jules-Vallés

Rue Jean-Henri Fabre

↙ Street stalls

Rue Lecuyer

Marché Jules-Vallés

Marché Aux Puces is in the northern district of Paris, St.Ouen

Transport: Tube - Take #4 Metro to Porte de Clignancourt.
  Bus - #56, 85, 137, 155, 166.

Days & Hours: Open Saturday, Sunday, Monday, 8 am – 6 pm.

Layout: Over 2000 stands filling a right angle of streets
  bordered by boulevard Péripherique & avenue Michelet.

The Marché Aux Puces started when the rag & bone men of
Paris were expelled from the city & settled near the Porte de
Clignancourt. The area became a haunt for professional junk men &
visitors looking for bargain antiques. Then in 1920, Romaine Vernaison, a
landowner, put up wooden sheds & rented them out to the junkmen. Now
the Puces is one of the largest flea markets in Europe, spread out over
125 acres, with 5 separate markets, plus pavement displays & arcades.
Each market is unique in character & ambience & offers every item
imaginable. For the best bargains go early Saturday morning with
the professional dealers. Sunday is too crowded & touristy. Monday
is quiet & prices may go down at closing time. Whenever you go
you're bound to find something amusing or interesting,
bargains of all kinds & a slice of Parisian life not en-
countered elsewhere.

MARCHÉ MALIK

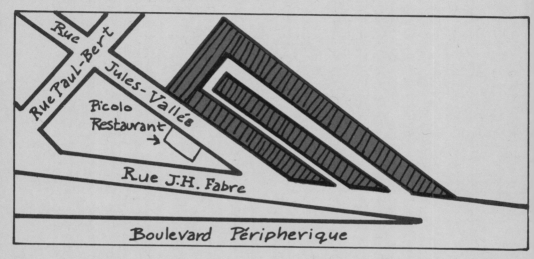

Rue Paul-Bert

Rue Jules-Vallés

Picolo Restaurant →

Rue J.H. Fabre

Boulevard Péripherique

Marché Malik is located between rue Jules-Vallés & rue J.H. Fabre & has about 60-80 stands. It was started by Prince Albanais, who opened a café in St. Ouen after traveling all over the world. The market is a hippy's paradise, with great bargains in clothing old & new for men, women & children - the latest from the Orient & Middle East, the Left Bank & the last war. Get friendly with a dealer & he'll put up a screen & let you try on whatever you want. You can even sell the coat off your back, if necessary! Also there are 40's kitsch & 30's Art Deco accessories, or do it yourself with beads & passementerie. Not to forget incense, henna, kohl & pot pipes. Go & enjoy.

Scavenger-hunt through bundled-up Old Clothes & find buried treasure, or buy them already cleaned & mended. Also New Clothes as found in Left Bank boutiques but at lower prices.

Antique Nightshirts cleaned & starched, some monogrammed.

Costumes, vestments, you name it—whatever you want to wear can be found in Malik.

Bushel baskets filled with Brass & Copper Fittings. This is the place to find that missing drawer pull, door knob, knocker, finger plate, lock or sconce.

GLACES
Parfums du Jour
Vanille
Chocolat
Noisette
Fraise
Citron
3 boules
pour 2^F

2^{F}50 LE DISQUE
5 pour 10^F

Records
At
Bargain Prices

Lots of Lions, fighting dogs, rearing horses — Bronzes — from the 19th C French school of Animalistes sculpture. Look closely for fine definition of eye, ears, etc. Is the piece signed? Beware of fakes, which are heavier & larger than originals.

Dégustation CAFE · RESTAURANT *Dégustation*
FRITE **A. PICOLO** MOULES

Have the specialty of the market: mussels & french fries with a glass of bière. Try the oysters in winter.

MARCHÉ JULES-VALLÉS

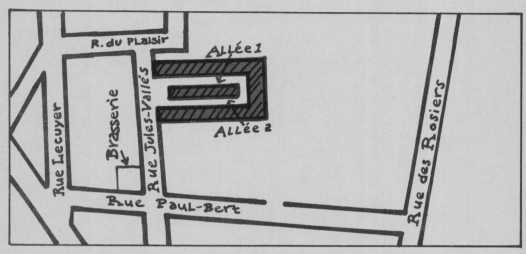

Marché Jules-Vallés, located at 7, rue Jules-Vallés, has 83 stands. It's a bit out of the way, but worth the trouble, especially since the street leading to it is lined with miscellaneous treasures. A casual, relaxed market, the dealers lounge about, not over interested in making a sale. It's filled with funny old things: 30's radios that still work, old postcards, Art Nouveau posters & accessories. You can find more substantial items as well, such as French clocks, bronzes, furniture & light fixtures. Bargains are to be had.

Lots of Clocks,
seen in the street &
in all the markets:
A French Mantel Pendule
from the late 19th C &
used to adorn the mantel
shelves of European fireplaces.

Comtoise Wall Clock →
Look for enamel dial with
repoussé brass case from the
mid 1800's. It can also be found
in a long case.

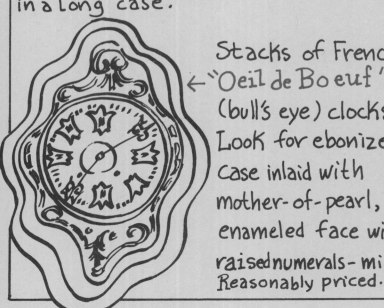

Stacks of French
← "Oeil de Boeuf"
(bull's eye) clocks.
Look for ebonized
case inlaid with
mother-of-pearl,
enameled face with
raised numerals - mid 19th C.
Reasonably priced.

ART NOUVEAU
Blown Glass Lamps

Shades & bases must be perfect, with no chips or cracks. Examine apertures & light fittings. Shade & base should match in shape, design, coloring.

ART DECO Lalique - glass
Lamps - Look for matt surfaces & pressed designs of flora, fauna & figures.

Glass Oil Lamps - Look
for double burners in the better lamps. Check that the base & top match, that the wick goes up & down, that the lamp actually works.

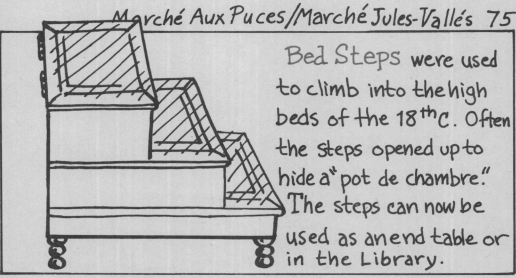

Bed Steps were used to climb into the high beds of the 18th C. Often the steps opened up to hide a "pot de chambre." The steps can now be used as an end table or in the Library.

Eat indoors or out or get snacks to walk in the street with, on the corner of rue Paul-Bert & rue Jules-Vallés.

MARCHÉ PAUL-BERT

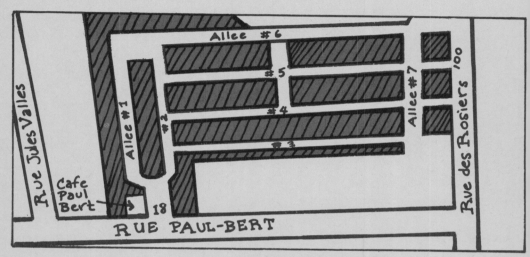

Allee #6

#5

#4

#3

Allee #1

Allee #2

Allee #7

100

Rue Jules Valles

Rue des Rosiers

Cafe
Paul
Bert

18

RUE PAUL-BERT

Marché Paul-Bert is located between 18, rue Paul-Bert & 100, rue de Rosiers & has over 250 stands. It's the newest market, begun after World War II. Large & spread out, the atmosphere is friendly & informal. There are numerous stands of French country-style furniture displayed as you would in your own home, down to the fresh flowers on the table. Also, other household items: lighting fixtures, chinaware, cookware, prints. Then the collector's items: small boxes & bibelots, orientalia, early machines, armor & arms, etc. Bargains are to be had.

Country Living with Rustic Furniture made of pine or oak. Look for armoires, farm tables, straw chairs. Smaller versions of these are more expensive. Least expensive are the straw chairs. In all the Paris markets.

Seen in the street: a Louis XV Commode (actually a chest of drawers). Most likely it's a recent copy- don't expect to find THE REAL THING in the Puces.

VICTORIAN Bamboo Furniture: canterburys, hat stands, side tables, etc. English, but very popular with the French.

Dutch Delft Tiles were hung in the ordinary man's home instead of paintings since the 17th c. Look for Landscapes, figures, animals.

French Copper Cookware Cul-de-poule, cocotte et casseroles - seen in the street for sale - may need a bit of polishing.

Ironware Mugs - what Parisians keep their coffee warm in because it holds the heat .5 fr. apiece, seen in the street & market.

Quimper Faïence - a style of provincial pottery with peasant scenes often on a yellow ground - perfect to go with your Rustic Furniture.

The Puces is where posh Parisians come to buy complete sets of Antique Silverware. Try Paul-Bert & particularly stand #144 in Biron. Old French silver is hard to come by - much was melted down during the Revolution.

Moulins à café et Mortiers -Coffee Mills The earliest were made in France in brass or iron Look for dovetailing in old wooden mills.

LE PAUL BERT CAFÉ

Specialités Maison
Profiterolles au Chocolat
Tartes: Fraises
Tatin
Rhubarbe

Stop for coffee & pastry at the gate of the market.

MARCHÉ BIRON

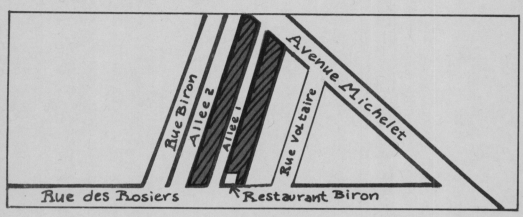

Rue des Rosiers · Rue Biron · Allee 2 · Allee 1 · Rue Voltaire · Restaurant Biron · Avenue Michelet

Marché Biron, located between 99, rue des Rosiers & 136, avenue Michelet, has over 200 stands & was started in 1925. It's the "rue St. Honoré" of the Puces-chic & rich, frequented by posh dealers & the snobs with their Vuitton bags. Most of the dealers are specialists & can be spotted by their velvet jackets. At lunchtime they hang netting over their wares & go off to Restaurant Biron for some of the best food in the Puces-to them good food is more important than sales. The stands in Biron are more like expensive antique shops, specializing in fine silver & china, arms, armor & nautical items, furniture, tapestries, bibelots, etc. Bargains are rare in Biron.

The French have been fond of Boxes of all Kinds since the court of Louis XIV. They're available in porcelain, enamel, tortoise shell, silver, in all the French markets. Boxes (with hinges) should spring open. Hold to the light to find holes & check the surface for dents, chips, splits.

Etui Boxes (containing everything for an 18th c manicure). Check - are all the contents there? Beware of new contents in an old box.

Limoges Porcelain Patch Boxes with ormolu hinge & catch. Make sure the closure is intact & working. More valuable boxes have designs on the inside lid as well.

Table Snuff Boxes made of papier mâché, decorated with historical portraits or events on the lid.

Plate Armor was designed not only to protect the wearer but to deflect blows & throw the striker off balance (note the ridge down the center of the breast plate) With the advent of gun powder in the 16th c armor became more ornate & was used only on festive occasions. Look for hallmarks of armorer.

Working models of Early Machines: steam engines, astrolabes, trains. Make sure the machine does what it's supposed to do. The smaller the model the more valuable it is.

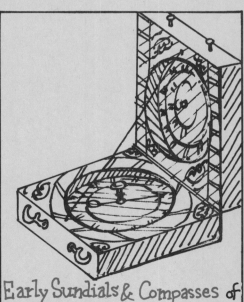

Early Sundials & Compasses of ivory or ebony are usually German-made. Fakes lack the fine detail of the originals.

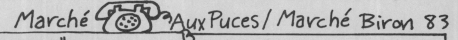

About Repro Furniture. The makers of reproduction furniture don't usually take much trouble with those areas not readily visible, such as the undersides of chairs & tables, the insides of drawers etc. Don't be afraid to ask the dealer to move the piece around. Look for newness of wood, recently glued joints, ornamentation that looks too bright. Watch out for wormholes - some dealers will deliberately maltreat an item to make it look old. Be suspicious when you see too much of an item or style in one area. Finally, ask for a receipt which clearly states the date made & not the style.

Stop at the best restaurant in the Puces for Lunch At 85, rue des Rosiers for pâté maison, tournedos béarnaise et tarte aux saison.

BAR
TÉL. CLI.03-06
LE BIRON

MARCHÉ VERNAISON

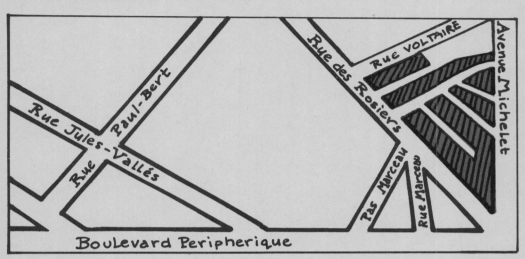

Marché Vernaison is located between 99, rue des Rosiers & 139, avenue Michelet, with over 300 stands. Vernaison is the biggest & oldest of the markets, started after World War I & named after its founder, Romaine Vernaison. It's perhaps the most interesting & amusing of all the markets — Le Vrai Puces. A treasure-trove of curiosities: old china dolls, funny old post cards, lace christening dresses, country farm tools & kitchen ware, oriental shoes for bound feet, sheriff's badges & holsters. Bargains are to be had.

Old Dolls are big in France. Look for leather or wooden bodies, wax or china heads, white elongated faces, earrings & ear holes. Brown eyes are rarer than blue. Dolls marked A.M. for Armand Marseille are German-made & not as valuable as French-made dolls.

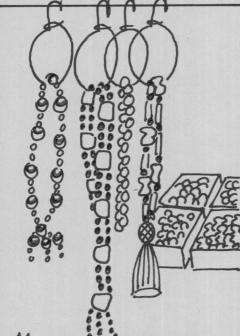

Make your own necklace from Boxes of Beads, spangles & sequins or buy ready-made About 7 Fr. a gobletful.

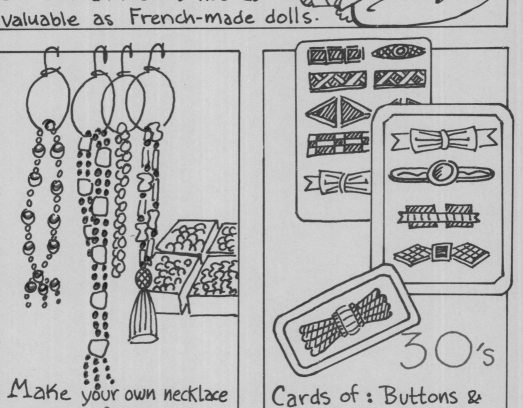

30's

Cards of : Buttons & Brooches, Buckles & Barrettes, Jet & Rhinestone, Frogs, Tassels

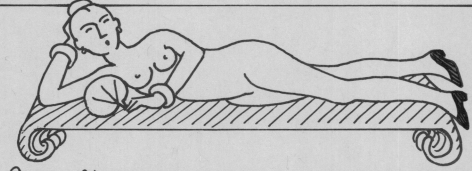

Since Chinese women never disrobed before strangers, when they were ill they used an ivory "Doctor's Lady" to point out to the doctor the part that ailed them.

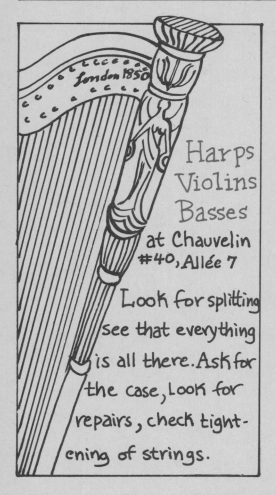

Harps
Violins
Basses
at Chauvelin
#40, Allée 7

Look for splitting see that everything is all there. Ask for the case, look for repairs, check tightening of strings.

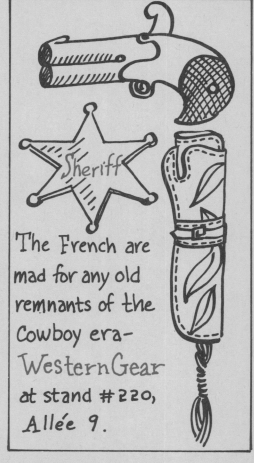

Sheriff

The French are mad for any old remnants of the Cowboy era - Western Gear at stand #220, Allée 9.

In 1872 the French government first authorized the use of the Post Card for correspondence. Lots of 20's bathing beauties & sweethearts to send to the folks back home at 1 Fr. apiece. Try stand #22, Allée 9.

Chez Louisette

At lunch-time go to the bistro where the dealers eat in Vernaison for a Kir 🍸 (white wine & crème de cassis), Live music & 🍸 singing.
Next to stand #244, allée 10, or 136, avenue Michelet.

VILLAGE SUISSE

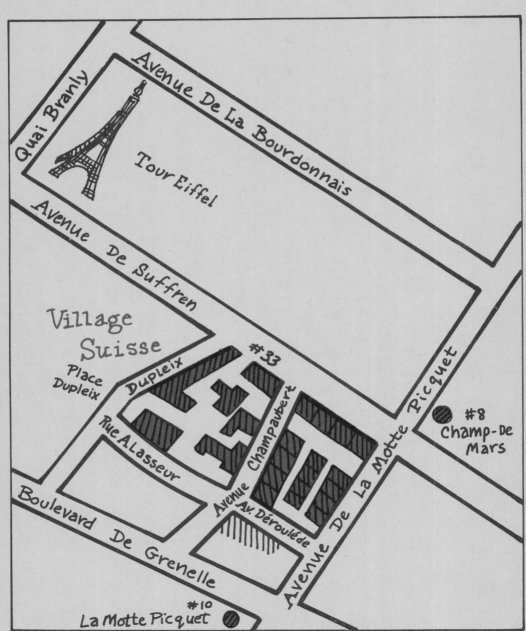

Quai Branly

Avenue De La Bourdonnais

Tour Eiffel

Avenue De Suffren

Village Suisse

Place Dupleix

Dupleix

#33

Champaubert

Avenue De La Motte Picquet

#8 Champ-De Mars

Rue A. Lasseur

Avenue Champaubert

Av. Déroulède

Boulevard De Grenelle

#10 La Motte Picquet

Village Suisse is in the 15th arrondisement on the Left Bank near the Eiffel Tower.

Transport: Tube- take the #8 or #10 metro to La Motte Picquet. Bus- take # 80 or # 82.

Days & Hours: Open everyday except Tuesdays & Wednesdays

Layout: Over 200 boutiques in the ground floor of an apartment building complex; also underground galleries.

The Village Suisse is neither a village nor Swiss, but it is laid out with gardens & fountains, each named after a Swiss town & the prices are definitely Swiss! The market started in 1900 at the time of the Paris Grand Exposition. Several years ago the area was razed & high-rise apartments were built. The market now occupies the ground floor level. The stands are really boutiques, elegant & chic, much like those in the Marché Biron. They tend to specialize in one area of collecting: antiquities, oriental items, Empire furniture, Gallé glass, etc. Many of the dealers are young & hip, often accompanied by a smart-looking dog. The clients are mostly posh dealers. Go & Look...

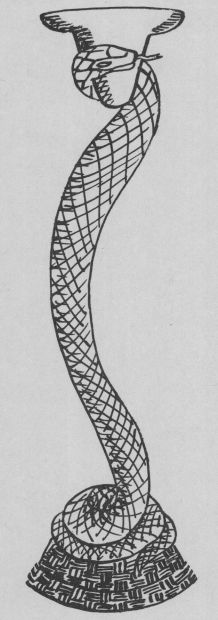

A Bronze Lamp by Edgar Brandt, an American in Paris in the 20's - famous for his cobras - expensive.

ART NOUVEAU Gallé Glass of the 1890's. Beware of reproductions! Never buy an unsigned piece - the signature should be part of the design.

Gallé

ART DECO Bronze Figures of acrobats, snake charmers, dog walkers. Look for ivory face & hands & a marble base.

ART NOUVEAU
Metal Objects ashtrays, Lamps, decorative pieces. ←Dragonfly Lady Lying on a Leaf seen at #36, Antonin Rispal, Place de Berne. Also try #13, allée 1 in Marché Biron for Art Nouveau.

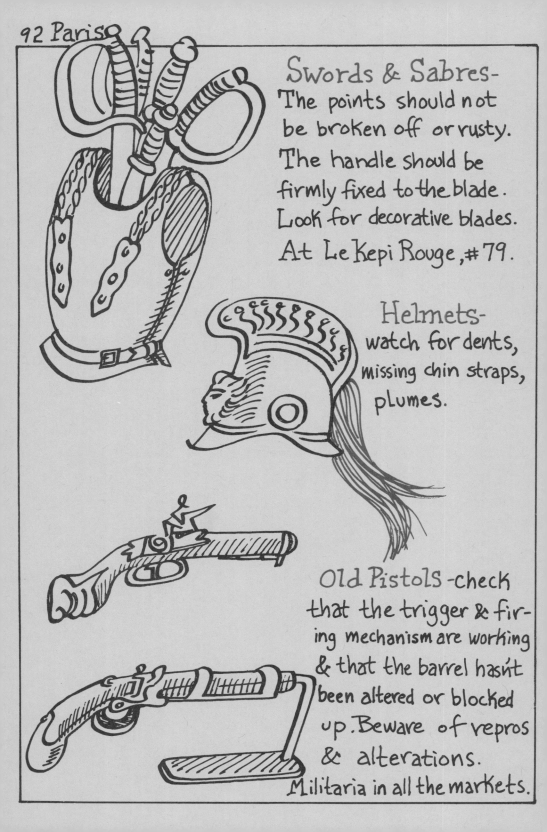

Swords & Sabres-
The points should not
be broken off or rusty.
The handle should be
firmly fixed to the blade.
Look for decorative blades.
At Le Kepi Rouge, #79.

Helmets-
watch for dents,
missing chin straps,
plumes.

Old Pistols -check
that the trigger & fir-
ing mechanism are working
& that the barrel hasn't
been altered or blocked
up. Beware of repros
& alterations.
Militaria in all the markets.

African Art from countries south of the Sahara, made of wood, ivory, stone or clay. It's very difficult to date these.

Minerals- agate, felspar, amethyst, make interesting desk pieces- Look for the attractiveness of the stone & varieties of color.

Prisoner-of-War Artifacts, Egg cups & table ornaments carved from nuts by prisoners at hard labor in the Cayenne Islands. Seen at Nicole Marty, #23, Allée de Suffren.

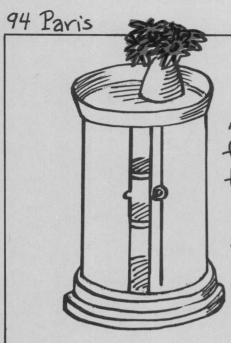

A brass Commode, formerly used to hold the "pot au chambre," makes an excellent small table or cupboard.

Barometers, strictly a scientific instrument at first, developed into a handsome wall ornament. The wooden rococo versions are the most sought after. Beware of buying the mercury type as they must be kept upright for shipping.

Armoires were originally used for storing arms but later became wardrobes as most European homes were built without closets. They can be converted to a bar or china closet, etc. Remember that early pieces were not designed to fit modern apartments & are grander in scale than newly made repros.

Fireplace Equipment in brass or bronze was unsurpassed in beauty during the latter half of the 18th c in France. Look for recent copies of fenders, firedogs.

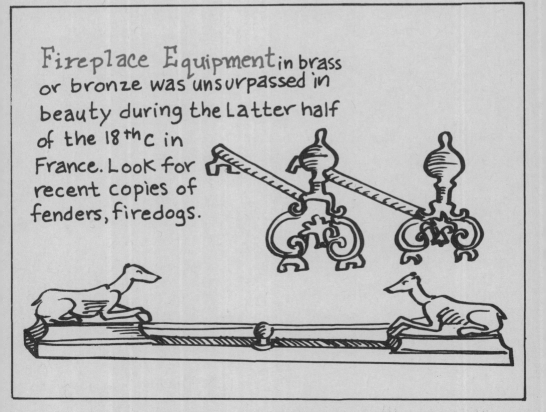

Oriental Snuff & Perfume Bottles - in ivory, jade, porcelain. The jade is the most valuable & should feel icy cold when pressed to the cheek. Check bottles for age - Look for wear marks on the base. There should be a stopper inside with a small spoon attached. Seen at Marco Polo, #87, on rue A Lasseur. Also at stand #145 in Marché Paul-Bert & the other Paris markets.

Netsuke are Japanese carved toggles made of wood, ivory or porcelain. Look for two holes used to hold the belt cord of an obi sash.

The designs are often folk-loric animals, figures or natural forms.

←for wine or tea

Chinese Cloisonné enamel ware is made by applying colored glass paste to a wired design on a metal base. The separated glazed colors give a brilliant effect on boxes, bowls, dishes

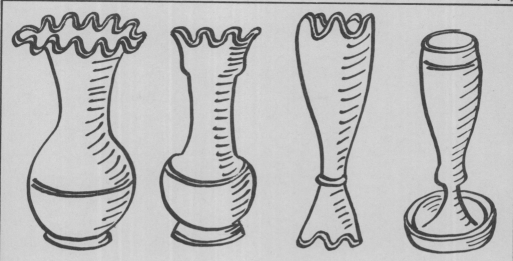

19th c Opaline Glass is a favorite with the French. It is translucent & comes in many shades of blue, pink, green & white. Look for the rare colors: turquoise, yellow & pigeon's blood. In all the Paris markets.

Go early & beat the dealer crowd or try Pub Suffren on avenue Suffren.

Some other Outdoor Markets

Porte de Lilas, Paris 20, Sundays.

Porte de Montreuil, Paris 11, Saturdays & Sundays.

Porte de Vanves, Paris 14, Saturdays & sundays.

Also

Go to the "Foire à la Ferraille" (the fair of old junk & scraps), a big antique fair held twice a year in Paris, 9 days before Palm Sunday & on the first saturday in October. It lasts for over 9 days & some 500 dealers as well as sellers of cooked meats show up for the big event. Check with the tourist office as to the Location.

Some Antiques Areas

On the Left Bank the area bordered by the Luxembourg Gardens & the

Seine on one side & the boulevard Saint-Michel & the rue du Bac on the other side. Walk down the rue de L'université - rue Jacob & all the little streets running off of them for some marvelous specialist shops.

The Right Bank: for the posh shops
rue de Berri, Paris 8.
rue Royale, Paris 8.
faubourg Saint-Honoré, Paris 8.
Place Vendôme, Paris 1.

Some Shippers in the Marché Aux Puces

Camard & Dimer, 140, rue de Rosiers, tel. 076-88-43.

W. Wingate & Johnston, Marché Biron in allée 1, tel. 202-77-10.

Société Nouvelle Atlantic, 62, rue Mirabeau, tel. 672-65-13.

Get the Guide Emer, published every two years by Éditions Emer. A European directory to Flea markets, antique shops, galleries, restorers, experts, shippers, etc. Available in Marché Biron at Raffy, stand #83.

Some Collections to See

Arms & Armor

Musée de l'armée, Hôtel des Invalides, Paris 7. Especially Napoleonic arms.

Furnishings

Musée des Arts Decoratifs, 107, rue de Rivoli—for furnishings, art objects & other applied arts.

Musée Nissim De Camondo, 63, rue de Monceau, Paris 8— contains some of the best 18th c furnishings.

Nautical

Musée de La Marine, Palais de Chaillot, Paris 16— everything for the nautical enthusiast.

Oriental

Musée Ceruschi, 7, avenue Vélasquez, Paris 8— Chinese & Japanese art.

Musée Guimet, 6, Place d'Iéna, Paris 16—one of the best displays of Far Eastern art.

NOTES

Names, Addresses of Dealers, Shops,
Restaurants, Prices paid, etc.

NOTES

ROME

PORTA PORTESE

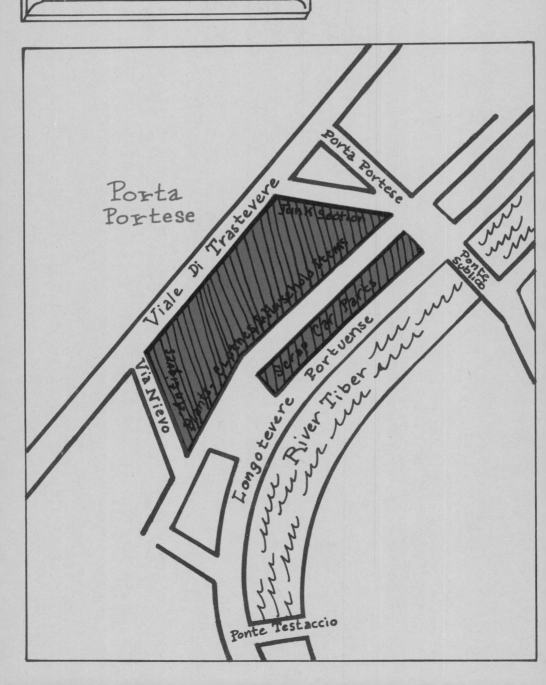

Porta Portese is in the Trastevere section of Rome by the Tiber River.

Transport: Take the #75 bus or a taxi.

Days & Hours: Open from midnight Saturday till 1 pm. Sunday.

Layout: Filling a triangle bordered by Viale di Trastevere, Via Portuense & Ponte Sublicio.

The Porta Portese arcade goes back to the Roman times of Urban VIII. The market is a melange of junk, antiques, plants, old & new clothes & God knows what else. Before dawn dealers & Roman connoisseurs search for the best items. At 10 the Sunday strollers arrive. Start in the junk section, known as "da'li zozzoni" (of the unwashed). Here dealers sit under beach umbrellas (take a sunhat), their treasures laid out in the dust, on old blankets or car hoods. Find: clocks & watches, old cameras, olive oil jugs & live music. Then bargain your way through the crowded clothes section into the tropical plants & finally the antiques. Here are buys in frames, furniture, church relics. But avoid reproductions! The market is lively, gay, picturesque, a bit like the boardwalk at Atlantic City - Go, enjoy & bargain!

Seen in the dirt, an Armillary Sphere, an early astronomical instrument. Look for several metal rings representing the circles of the celestial sphere – a handsome desk accessory.

Seeing Double?
Look out for:
fake watches
fake cigarettes
fake antiquities
fake records
fake gypsies with
fake babies
fake orange drink...

Old Telephones that can be hooked up to work. Old Cameras also. Make sure it's lightproof with no holes in the case & that everything works.

Religious Reliquaries receptacles for bits of nails, hair & bone of the saints.

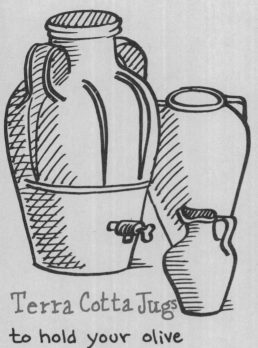

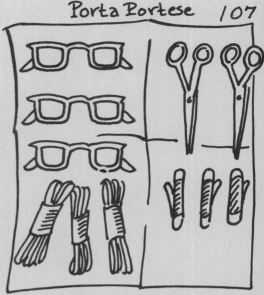

Terra Cotta Jugs to hold your olive oil or wine.

Scattered on the ground- Notions used & unused, also old clocks, old shoes, bird cages, etc.

Clocks & Watches on car hoods, diamonds in the dust, treasures on the back of trucks, reliquaries on old blankets under umbrellas-take your pick!

Lots of Army Gear, fatigues, backpacks, sailor shirts, etc.

20's Fashion Plate Post Cards

"Chestnuts Roasting on an open fire" with a Chestnut Burner that keeps them from burning. Also: coffee grinders, nut crackers, & other Kitchen gadgets. Inexpensive.

Giant Striped Country Umbrellas hard to come by.

Enormous Tropical Plants separate the antiques & clothes sections.

Leather Goods than the boutiques.

of all Kinds at prices lower

Saints flambé,
Bits of Statues of saints & sinners
from churches in the South.

When buying IKons
check: Is it painted or
printed? Is all the detail
work undamaged? Look for
indication of age & origin at
the top or bottom near the
edge. Beware of fakes.

Records, some of them
pornographic. Check
that the contents
match the cover.

Frames at reasonable prices

all sizes
&
all shapes

Silver Plate is very big in Italy - most of it comes from England, where plate marks were made to look like silver hall marks - but note no Lion!

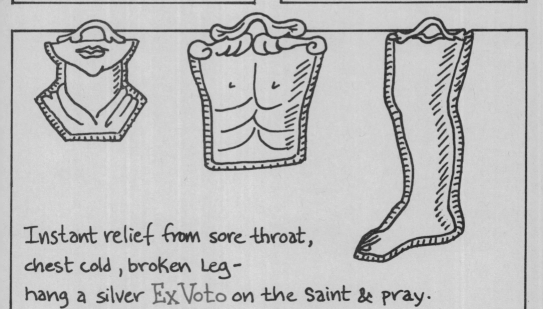

Instant relief from sore throat, chest cold, broken Leg - hang a silver Ex Voto on the Saint & pray.

Bits of Ornamental Stone Carving &
Wood Carving - Folk Art from Sicilian
chariots- good for wall hangings

Bread Baskets,
Laundry Baskets,
Picnic Baskets,
& other straw accessories.

Antiquities- nice for
paper weights, but don't spend
a lot on them- if they're
any good, they're in museums;
if not, they're copies.

More foods to walk
the street with

Eat freshly peeled
prickly pears →

PAGNOTTELLE
L. 150

Buy paper cones of
olives and beans & chunks
of sliced coconuts.

ALSO IN ROME

Other Markets: Piazza de Fontanella Borghese near via Condotti, monday through Saturday, for fine antiques & paintings.

Antiques Areas: via del Babuino, via Margutta & Via Coronari.

Collections to See for

Arms & Armor- Castello Sant'Angelo, in Piazza Adriana & Palazzo Venezio.

Carved Wooden Figures- Palazzo Venezio on via de Plebiscito.

Coins & Medals- Museo Nazionale on via Volterna.

Furnishings- Palazzo Quirinale on via del Quirinale.

Rugs & Carpets - Museo Vaticano (the Sistine Chapel, Palaces & galleries).

Silver & Goldsmith's Work- Tesoro della Basilica di San Pietro (the Vatican).

NOTES

Names, Addresses of Dealers, Shops, Restaurants, Prices paid, etc.

NOTES

FLORENCE

PIAZZA DEI CIOMPI

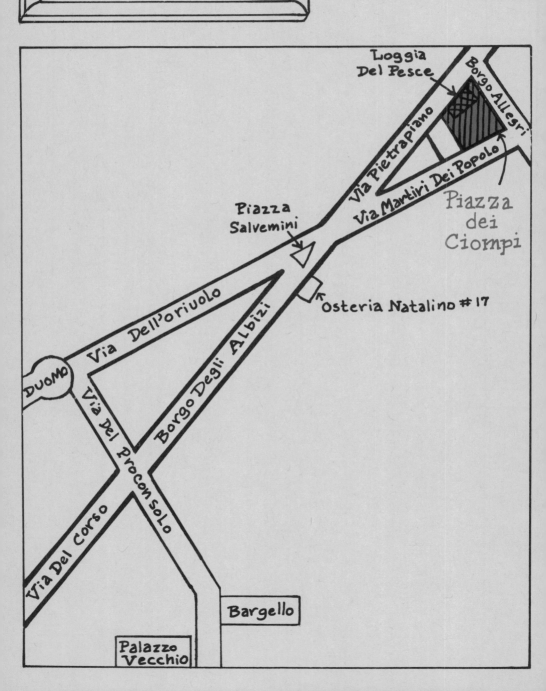

Loggia Del Pesce

Borgo Allegri

Via Pietrapiano

Via Martiri Dei Popolo

Piazza dei Ciompi

Piazza Salvemini

Via Dell'oriuolo

Borgo Degli Albizi

Osteria Natalino #17

DUOMO

Via Del Proconsolo

Via Del Corso

Bargello

Palazzo Vecchio

Piazza dei Ciompi is next to the Loggia del Pesce on Via Piatrapiano down from the Post Office.

Transport: Walk or take a taxi.

Days & Hours: Everyday but Sunday, 9 – 5.

Layout: The market consists of about 25 covered sheds closely grouped in an open square.

Piazza dei Ciompi is a small, compact, antique, covered market in an open square surrounded by old palazzos. It's next to the Loggia del Pesce, once a fish market built by Vasari around 1568. Notice the attractive fish seals  on the arcades. It's a fun market filled with odd bits & pieces, bric-a-brac, religious items, prints, pottery, some furniture, light fixtures, & lots of copper & brass. The market is good for a poke around on the odd afternoon or morning & you may find the unexpected treasure.

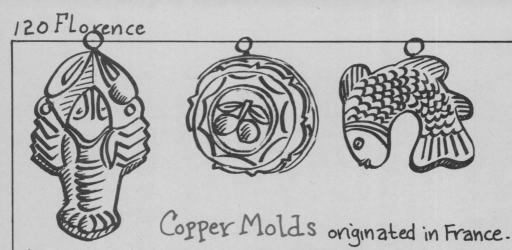

Copper Molds originated in France. Make sure they're solid copper, not a plated alloy. Request to make a small scratch on the bottom with a penknife & look carefully at the edges. Old molds should have a hard deep shine & small dents & scratches from wear.

Attractive brass or wrought iron Plant Stands.

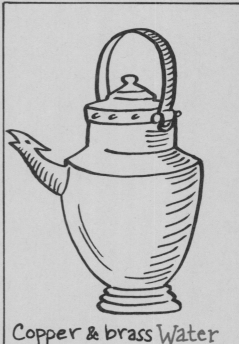

Copper & brass Water Carriers copies of a traditional Renaissance pot.

Witch's Cauldron
for the occultist.

A wide variety of
Flatirons & their
stands, which held the
hot coals - they make
decorative doorstops.

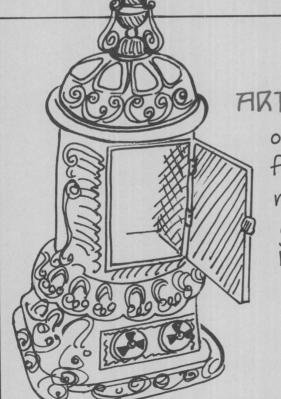

ART NOUVEAU Ironware
of all kinds - wood
furnaces, bed steads,
mirrors & frames,
glass & wrought iron
light fixtures, etc.

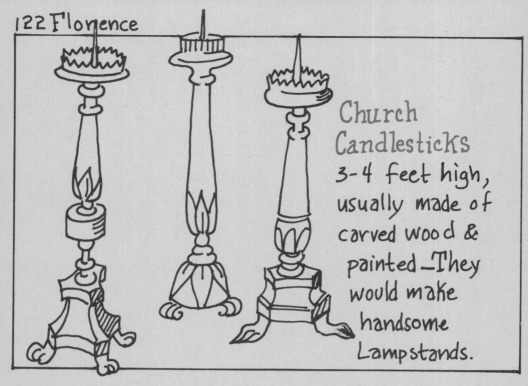

Church Candlesticks 3-4 feet high, usually made of carved wood & painted — They would make handsome Lampstands.

Glass Chandeliers probably from Venice. Find out if it's crystal, which reflects the light more softly than glass.

Decorative Metal Frames from churches

Take home a
Coat of Arms or
family seal in
ceramic, painted
wood or metal—
makes a decorative
wall hanging.

Florentine Savonarola
Folding Chairs
Most seen will be
copies of Renaissance
designs, carved in wood
with mother-of-pearl
inlay. Look for large
rings on the arms for
nervous Florentines to
fiddle with.

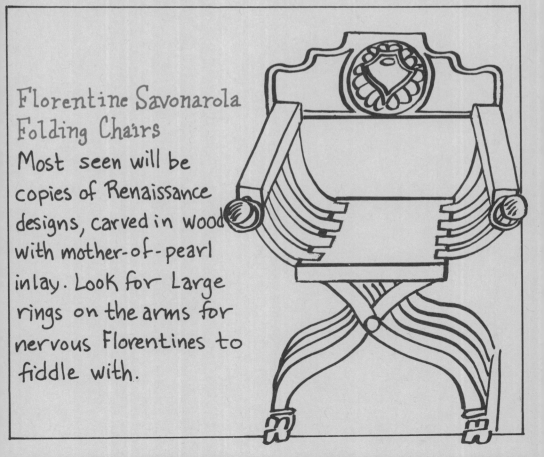

For the Hat fancier,
fetishist or collector - a wide selection
at bargain prices.

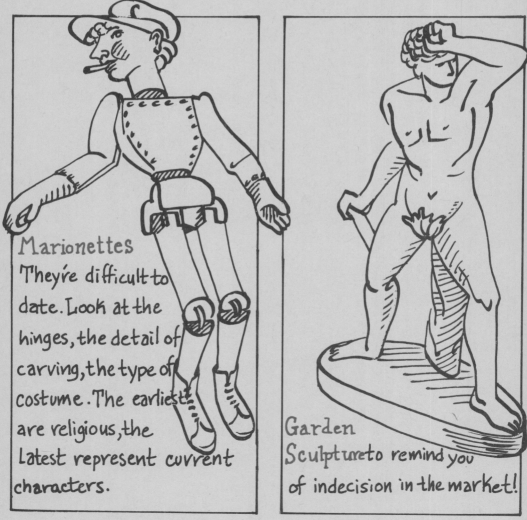

Marionettes
They're difficult to
date. Look at the
hinges, the detail of
carving, the type of
costume. The earliest
are religious, the
latest represent current
characters.

Garden
Sculpture to remind you
of indecision in the market!

BRIC-A-BRAC
ENTRATE
LIBRE
• ET •
ACQUISTATE

STAND N. 18

A hodge-podge of funny, odd bits & pieces, bric-a-brac, tobacco boxes, prints, embroidered Easter eggs, coffee grinders, Art Nouveau bedsteads, old cameras, Lace chemises, etc. Scare-crow man made of miscellaneous treasures at Stand 18.

IL · GUSCIO
INGRESSO LIBERO
DA · BUFERA

Large, decorative painted tin Feast Crowns from some holiday procession or other. Religious festival & church decorations at reasonable prices.

Italian tin-glazed wares known as Faïence in the market are mostly copies of Renaissance-style pottery. Note the influence of Hispano-Moresque floral & geometric patterns.

Small glazed Sculptures, probably of some religious subject.

For a good hearty Lunch go to
Osteria Natalino
Via Borgo degli Albizi, 17

Have the regional
dish: tuna with
white beans &
figs & prosciutto
in season.

ALSO IN FLORENCE

Other Markets: The Straw market in the Loggia De Porcellino for inexpensive gifts.

Antiques Area : Via Maggio

Collections to see for

Arms & Armor- Museo Stibbert, via Federico Stibbert, #26.

Clocks & Watches-Museo di Storia della Scienza, Piazza dei Giudici, #1.

Furniture-Galleria degli Uffizi at Piazza degli Signorinia. Also Palazzo Davanzati on via Porta Rossa, #9, which houses the Museo della Casa Fiorentina - a collection of 14th, 15th & 16th C furnishings.

Gold & Silversmith's work-Museo degli Argenti, Piazza Pitti, Palazzo Pitti.

Every 2 years (1971, 1973) there's an international exhibition of antiques from mid-September to mid- October at the Palazzo Strozzi, Piazza Strozzi.

NOTES

Names, Addresses of Dealers, Shops, Restaurants, Prices paid, etc.

NOTES

MADRID

EL
RASTRO

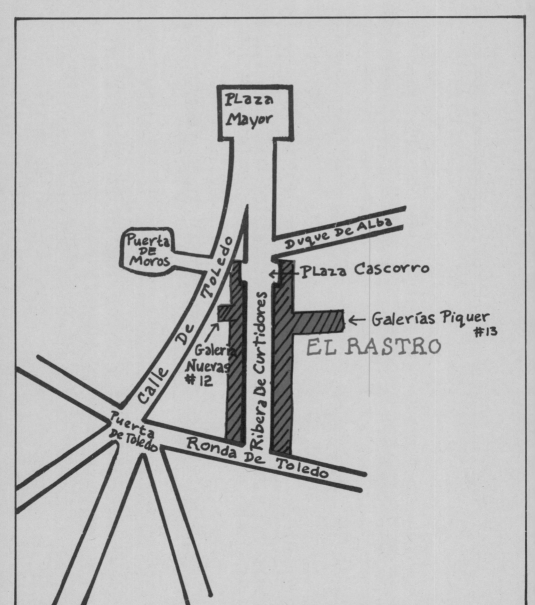

Plaza Mayor

Puerta DE Moros

Duque De Alba

Plaza Cascorro

Calle De Toledo

Ribera De Curtidores

← Galerías Piquer
#13

Galería Nuevas #12

EL RASTRO

Puerta De Toledo

Ronda De Toledo

EL Rastro begins around the Plaza del Cascorro, continues down the Ribera de Curtidores & ends at the Rondo de Toledo in the southern section of the city.

Transport: Take a taxi.

Days & Hours: Open everyday 9am-9pm, but Sunday is best.

Layout: Over 1,000 stalls, shops & arcades, spread down one main avenue.

EL Rastro is like Portobello Road, one long avenue of shops, stalls & pavement displays, but it's double the width & longer. The street is filled with 4 teeming lanes of human traffic. Off the main promenade are galerías of small posh shops built around a court yard, 2 or 3 stories high. In here you'll find the better quality stuff. Back on the street are stalls selling everything from freshly cooked lobster claws to lace mantillas, paella pots, copper warming pans, gaucho boots, Moroccan leather goods & God knows what else. In the galerías are manuscripts, prints, paintings, silver, reliquaries, furniture, carved doors, etc. Go when the locals go for their Sunday outing. Drink beer & eat "tapas" (Spanish snacks) in the cafeterias around the Plaza. Bargains to be had.

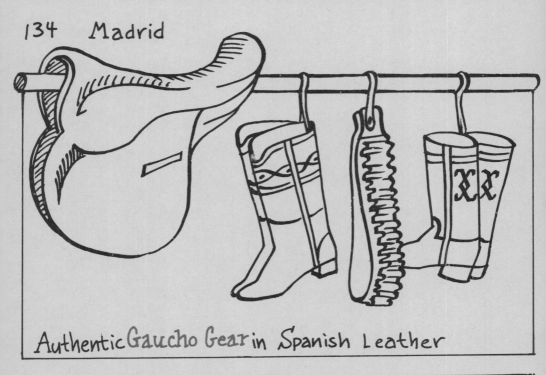

Authentic Gaucho Gear in Spanish Leather

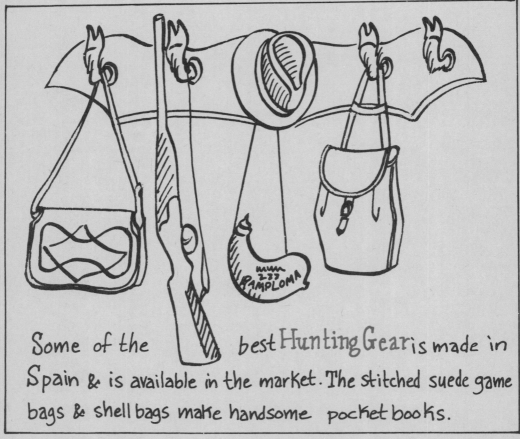

Some of the best Hunting Gear is made in Spain & is available in the market. The stitched suede game bags & shell bags make handsome pocket books.

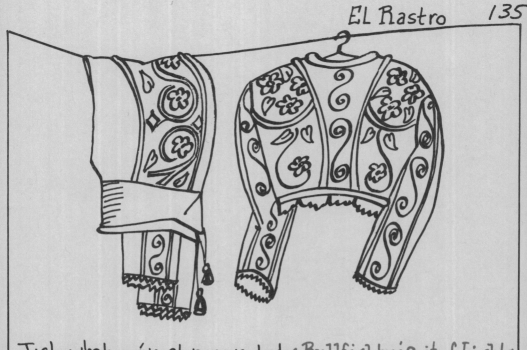

Just what you've always wanted - a Bullfighter's suit of Lights

Handmade Spanish Lace, mantillas, embroidered
shawls hanging in the street.

Copperware by the ton – warming pans, pitchers, mixing bowls, Ladles, etc. Check that they're solid copper.

Albarellos or Apothecary Jars
The cylindrical shape is Middle-Eastern & came into Spain with the Moorish invasion. In the 15th C the jars were made of ceramic & later of glass, to hold herbs, powders & unguents.

Painted Trays of enameled tin or papier mâché, or Lacquered. The papier maché is lighter in weight & longer lasting (the tin trays tend to chip). Look for crazing in older trays.

Maiolica Pottery is earthenware with a tin-enamel glaze. The painted decorations (in cobalt blue, green, yellow, orange on a white ground) are distinctly Moorish in design.

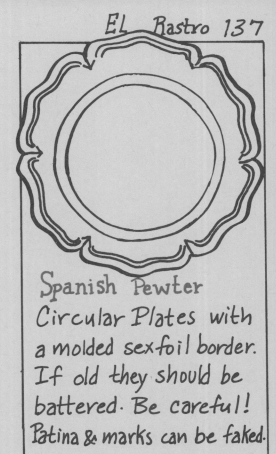

Spanish Pewter Circular Plates with a molded sexfoil border. If old they should be battered. Be careful! Patina & marks can be faked.

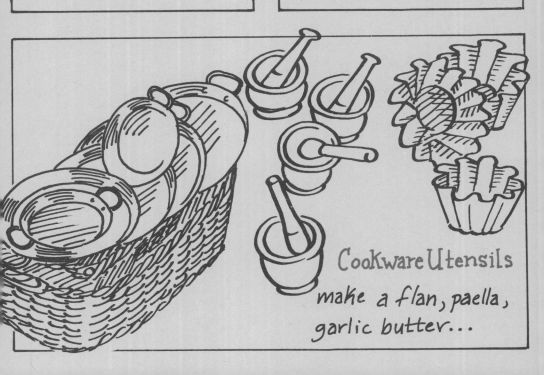

Cookware Utensils

make a flan, paella, garlic butter...

Lots of recently made copies of
Renaissance-style Furniture at
reasonable prices. Also older more expensive
copies from the 19thC in the galerias.

Carved & Gilt-framed Mirrors
If they're old the backs should
be silvery with black spots &
have beveled edges.

19thC Hall Chairs with
the family coat of arms
carved on the back. These hard
wooden chairs were used by
errand boys waiting in the hall.

Bow →

Shank →

Bit →

Gothic Keys - Look for plain & simple design. Renaissance Keys are much more elaborate. (French are the finest.)

Wrought Ironware

window grilles, chapel screens, gateways, all show the influence of Moorish linear design

Decorative stone Garden Sculpture

in alabaster or marble. Should be smooth & heavy.

Religious Sculpture - carved wooden cherubs - often taken from clusters of cherubim. It's difficult to tell how old church sculpture is - anywhere from 50-100 years old. Most of it came on the market after the Civil War.

Illuminated Manuscripts made in the monasteries for the Church & the court. The more valuable ones have colorful images & decorative motifs.

imaculata non in justification ut non confunda

Church Altar Sticks brass. Early sticks were hollow. 19thc were cast solid in one piece.

Street Snacks in the Market

Buy cooked Lobster claws & crabs

Eat in the street: Candy apples &

Cones of salted almonds

Or eat "Tapas" (spanish snacks) & drink beer in a cafeteria

ALSO IN MADRID

Antiques Areas: Vara del Rey or Ribera de Curtidores.

Collections to See

Arms & Armor - Museo de La Real Armeria next to the Palazzo Real.

Coins, Enamel, Gold & Silversmith's Work- The Prado at Paseo del Prado. Also the Museo de Lázaro Galdiano on calle de Serrano, # 122.

Decorative Folk Arts - Artes Decorativas on calle de Montalban, # 12.

Furnishings- The Palazzo Real, Plaza de Oriente. Museo Romántico on calle de San Mateo, # 13.

Nautical Items- Ministerio de Marino Y Museo Naval on calle de Montalban, # 2.

NOTES

Names, Addresses of Dealers, Shops,
Restaurants, Prices paid, etc.

NOTES

·Points to Consider when Buying an Item·

1. Is the item all there? *No repairs, no damages, no marrying?*
2. Does it show the wear & tear of years of use? Look on the bottom, back or along the edges.
3. Does it do what it's supposed to do? (i.e., clock- keep time)
4. Is it made of the correct material? Is it the same size as the original, the right color & weight?
5. Is it signed by its maker, hallmarked or otherwise identifiable as to date, place or maker?
6. Has it got fine definition of detail—or is it a blurred copy of the original as repros often are?
7. Is it characteristic of its type or an unusual variation?
8. Is it pretty?

Don't let greed overcome caution—if you're not sure about something, don't buy it!

Collector's Test Kit

The Touch Test

On dishes, run your hands along the edges in a circular motion to feel for cracks or chips.

to test Porcelain

Bong!

Rap the side sharply with the knuckles. The porcelain dish should give a nice long ring. If the is no ring, the piece is cracked. If it's a short ring, it's been repaired.

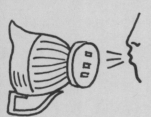

Breathe on Silver to make hallmarks show up clearly & to reveal repairs. This also works on repaired china.

Take a high-power Magnifying Glass for looking at gem stones, hallmarks, cameos - wear it on a string around your neck.

Turn most items upside down (furniture, china, silver) to look for wear on the bottom!

Carry a ⬭ PenKnife to test jade. Make a small scrape on the bottom- if it scratches easily, it's soapstone. Press jade to your lips - it should feel icy regardless of the weather.

Bring a ⬭ Nailfile to scratch the bottom of porcelain. If it's soft paste porcelain it should scratch easily; if not, it's hard paste. Also note, porcelain is light & dainty, while pottery is usually heavy & thick.

Dampen the end of a ⬭ caustic Pencil & rub on a supposed silver item. The item will change color if it's not silver.

Buy a Spring Balance to weigh silver items by troy ounces - remember it must be held vertical.

Don't forget to Ask for a ⬭ Winding Key when you buy a clock or watch.

☞ Caveat Emptor - "Let the buyer beware" of any item in too good condition, too shiny or too cheap. It may be either "repro", doctored-up, over-restored or stolen & its value will be considerably reduced.

·About Dealers, Dealing & Prices·

☞ Where do the Dealers get their wares?

From other dealers-a single item may change hands 5 times in one morning.

From "call outs"- calls from private parties who want to sell a few items in their houses.

From "house clearances"-at which the entire contents of a house is sold for one set price.

From the public-who bring individual items into their shops.

From auctions.

From country antique fairs & church jumble sales-the dealers go early & buy up everything of value.

From "runners"- who buy from one dealer & sell to another for a small commission.

☞ How much Profit do Dealers make?

The market trader is interested only in a quick turnover & settles for a small profit margin of 10-20%. The antique shop owner has a greater overhead & must make a profit margin of 50-100% on a sale.

☞ The Best Prices are offered at opening time when the dealer is eager to make his first sale of the day & at closing time when he's glad to have less to drag home.

☞ Prices Vary from stall to stall, market to market, country to country, season to season & are subject to constant fluctuation caused by supply & demand, monetary inflation, fashion, etc.

☞ Remember the marked price is not the final price! A dealer often has his own marking system to determine the lowest he can go & still make a profit. For example in London one dealer's method-🏷10£x the price plus an x means he's willing to knock 1£ off the price. Two xs means 2£ off.

☞ Don't be put off by dust, dirt or tarnishes on silver or other goods in the market. The same item shined up on display in a posh shop may often cost 30-60% more than you'd pay here!

☞ Request a Descriptive Invoice on any expensive purchases, with the approximate date of manufacture, etc.

·Market Lingo & Dealer's Jargon·

Antiquaire- (Fr.)-A licensed dealer who sells only authentic antiques.

Bent Stuff -(Eng.) Stolen wares.

British Antique Dealer's Association Ltd. 20, Rutland Gate, London, W7. Write for list of some 500 dealers who sell only authentic antiques.

Brocanteur- (Fr.) Licensed French dealer in bric-a-brac, junk, antiques.

Brocante -(Fr.) Bric-a-brac, junk, etc.

To Bunk in-(Eng.) To throw in another item in a sale.

Call Bird-(Eng.) An unusual item a dealer places on his stall to attract attention.

To Catch a Cold (Eng.) To buy in error, a 'wrong' piece for too much money.

Chambre Syndicale des Experts Professionnel- 52, rue Taitbout, Paris. Association of experts who authenticate & value antiques.

Les Chineurs- (Fr.) The junkmen.

Dans leurs jus -(Fr.) "In their juice"- antiques that have not been restored.

Dealer, general -(Eng.) Buys & sells anything for a profit.

Dealer, Specialist - Specializes in one particular area of antiques.

Dealer's Market - Where shop owners & other dealers go to buy at trade prices.

To Distress an Item - To make an item look older than it actually is.

To Drop it a Bit - To lower the price.

Fakes - Counterfeit items passed off as originals.

Flogging - Selling.

Gear - Trade term for merchandise.

Hybrid - Like marrying, the joining of two or more different parts often with the intent to deceive.

Knocker - A dealer who goes from door to door with a bundle of "fivers" offering to buy anything that's for sale.

Lovely Kip - (Eng.) when an item is in good shape.

Marrying - (Eng.) joining one piece to another from perhaps a different period.

Pricey - (Eng.) Expensive.

Reproduction - An exact copy of a piece from an earlier period. Sometimes details may be left out or the scale changed to fit modern apartments' size.

Reproduction, Authentic - An acknowledged authorized line-for-line copy of an original piece.

Ribby- When an item's authenticity or condition is suspect.

Runner- A man who buys merchandise from one dealer & tries to sell it to another dealer.

Smalls- Small items, Knick-knacks.

Stall (Eng.), Stand (Fr.)- A dealer's display area.

Steep- Expensive.

Totters- Dealers.

Totty- Dealer's gear, usually in the junk category.

Trade Price The lowest "wholesale" price on an item.

Some Dealer's Classified Customers

B. & O.ers- Box openers.

L. & L.ers - Lifters & Lookers.

P.U.& P. D.ers- Picker uppers & putter downers.

S. & S.ers - Sniffers & sneerers.

T. W.- Time-wasters asking endless questions.

Tabbers- Someone who tabs around (prowls) looking for bottomless bargains.

Twisted Knickers- someone who pilfers.

Some Comments a Dealer doesn't want to hear

About the rarest item on the dealer's stall, "How much is this? We've got one at home...." or "Oh look, we threw

one of those away last year."
About a matching pair of items, "too
bad, I only wanted one..."

Or a customer picks up a genuine item
& says "Pity it's a reproduction, dear"
or "it would be lovely if it was all there..."
The Best Policy - Examine the item with
care, practice your English (Fr., It., Sp.)
accent & don't say too much.

·Bibliography·

The bibliography that follows represents a selection of books used by the author & recommended to those who wish to delve further into the details & history of the objects shown. Some are inexpensive English paperbacks you can pick up in your travels or find here. Others are good general guides to the broad areas of antiques.

Paperback

Robert Nicholson's <u>Nicholson's Collectors' London</u> (London, Robert Nicholson Publications) is an excellent pocket-size guide full of addresses of London dealers, shops, museums, shippers, societies, restorers.

Guy William's <u>Collecting Cheap China & Glass</u>, <u>Collecting Silver & Plate</u>, <u>Collecting Victoriana</u>, <u>The Home-Lovers' Guide to Antiques & Bric-a-Brac</u> are a series of small, useful & informative Corgi minibooks published by Transworld, London.

The <u>Discovering</u> series is published by Shire, Tring, Herts., England. Some sample titles: <u>Discovering Hallmarks in English Silver</u> by John Bly; <u>Discovering Militaria</u> by Peter Newman; <u>Discovering Smoking Antiques</u> by Amoret & Christopher Scott.

Hamlyn All-Color Paperbacks, many of them published in the United States by Bantam Books, are profusely illustrated. Look for: Antique Furniture by Plantagenet Somerset Fry; Clocks & Watches by Kenneth Ullyett; Porcelain by Eileen Aldridge; Pottery by Henry Hodges.

Hardcover

John Bedford's series: Looking in Junk Shops, Still Looking for Junk & More Looking in Junk Shops, published in London by Macdonald & Co. This is an excellent series with newsy tidbits & illustrations of many inexpensive items.

The Collectors' Pieces series is published by Cassell in London. Some titles: John Bedford's Bristol, Delftware, Pewter, Staffordshire, Small Boxes.

Some Big General Guides

The Complete Encyclopedia of Antiques, compiled by Connoisseur magazine, Hawthorn Books.

Plantagenet Somerset Fry, The World of Antiques, Hamlyn, 1970.

George Savage, The Antique Collector's Handbook, Spring Books, New York & London, 1968.

Marvin D. Schwartz & Betsy Wade, The New York Times Book of Antiques, New York, Quadrangle Books, 1972.

Annual Publications

The British Antiques Yearbook, London, S.J. Phillips, Ltd.

Guide Emer, Paris, Editions Emer. A yearly guide & directory for antiquarians of addresses of shops, restorers, markets, etc.

The International Antiques Yearbook, New York, Ralph M. Chait Galleries.

The Lyle Official Antiques Review, compiled & edited by R.A. Curtis & M.J. Miller, Sussex, Lyle Publications.

· Index ·